HANDS-ON HISTORY

AZTECS

DRESS, EAT, WRITE, AND PLAY JUST LIKE THE AZTECS

FIONA MACDONALD

QEB Publishing

Library of Congress Control Number:
2007000935

ISBN 978 1 59566 351 1

Written by Fiona Macdonald
Editor Felicity Fitchard
Designer Liz Wiffen
Projects made by Veronica Erard

Publisher Steve Evans
Creative Director Zeta Davies
Senior Editor Hannah Ray

Printed and bound in China

Picture credits

Key: T = top, B = bottom, C = center, L = left, R
= right,
FC = front cover

The Art Archive: p. 4 tl: Government Palace
Tiaxcala Mexico/Dagli Orti; p. 6 tr: Museo Ciudad
Mexico/Dagli Orti; p. 6 br: Dagli Orti; p. 8 tl: Museo
Ciudad Mexico/Nicolas Sapieha; p. 8 br, p. 14 tr, p.
18 cl: Museo del Templo Mayor Mexico/Dagli Orti;
p. 10tr, p. 28 tr: Biblioteca Nacional Mexico/Dagli
Orti; p. 12 tl: Mireille Vautier; p. 12 br; p. 14 cb: Bibli-
othéque des Arts Décoratifs Paris/Dagli Orti; p. 16
tr: Antochiw Collection Mexico/Mireille Vautier; p.
16 bl: Museum Für Völker Kunde Vienna/Dagli Orti;
p. 18 ct; p. 18 br: Biblioteca Nacional Madrid/Dagli
Orti; p. 20 tl: Mireille Vautier; p. 20 br: National
Anthropological Museum Mexico/Dagli Orti; p. 22 tl:
Mireille Vautier; p. 24 tl: Dagli Orti.

Bridgeman Art Library: p. 11 tr: Mexican School
(16th century)/Museo de America, Madrid, Spain;
p. 23 tr: Mexican School (20th century)/Archives
Charmet, Private Collection;
p. 26 bl: Spanish School (16th century)/Biblioteca
Medicea-Laurenziana, Florence, Italy.

Corbis: p. 26 tr: Bob Krist.

Werner Forman Archive: FC: Biblioteca
Universitaria, Bolognia, Italy; p. 4 br, p. 24 br:
British Museum, London;
p. 28 bl: Liverpool Museum, Liverpool.

Words in **bold** are explained
in the glossary on page 30.

Web site information is correct at the time
of going to press. However, the publishers
cannot accept liability for any information
or links found on third-party Web sites.

Before undertaking an activity which
involves eating or the preparation of food,
parents and/or teachers should ensure
that none of the children in their care
are allergic to any of the ingredients.
In a classroom situation, prior written
permission from parents may be required.

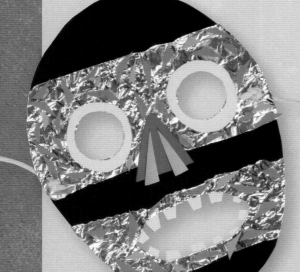

CONTENTS

WHO WERE THE AZTECS?

The Aztecs ruled an empire in Mesoamerica, the land between North and South America. Before they grew powerful around 700 years ago, many different civilizations flourished and built cities in this region, including the **Toltecs** and **Maya**. Each of these peoples had its own laws, skills, and traditions, but they also shared many religious beliefs and ways of running their communities. The Aztecs learned from the ideas, knowledge, and skills of these earlier peoples and built a civilization that **dominated** Mesoamerica for almost 200 years.

◄ An Aztec man (right) and woman (left) say prayers in front of a holy statue. This picture was painted 500 years after the Aztecs lived, but shows us what they looked like.

Mesoamerica (Central America) is shown in yellow here. Tenochtitlan was the Aztecs' capital city. ►

DID YOU KNOW?

THE AZTECS' OWN NAME FOR THEMSELVES WAS THE "MEXICA." TODAY, WE STILL USE THIS NAME FOR THEIR HOMELAND, MEXICO.

EARLY BEGINNINGS

At first, the Aztecs were poor, wandering hunters, struggling to survive in the dry desert land of North Mexico. But around 1200 C.E. they migrated south, to the Central Valley of Mexico. They found water, animals, and plants—and other people already living there! The Aztecs were not made welcome.

GAINING POWER

For 100 years, the Aztecs worked for the Valley peoples as soldiers and slaves. Around 1300 C.E., they rebelled and seized power. They grew rich and strong and conquered nearby lands. They forced the people they had conquered to give them tribute (tax) such as food, clothes, gold, and treasure.

▲ An Aztec pendant shaped like a two-headed poisonous snake. It is made of turquoise (a semi-precious stone) with carved shells for teeth.

MAKE A TWO-HEADED SERPENT STAMP

Snakes were a symbol of the Aztec god Quetzalcoatl (Keht-tsal-coh-ah-tl). His name means "feathered serpent."

YOU WILL NEED:
TWO RECTANGLES OF CARDBOARD • PENCIL • TRACING PAPER • CRAFT KNIFE • GLUE • WHITE, GREEN, AND BLUE ACRYLIC PAINT • SAUCER • PAINTBRUSH OR ROLLER • FINE PAINTBRUSH • WHITE PAPER

1 Trace the two-headed snake onto one of the cardboard rectangles. Ask an adult to cut it out with a craft knife.

2 To make your stamp, glue the snake shape to the other card rectangle. Leave to dry completely.

3 Mix up some turquoise paint. Roll or brush paint evenly over the snake shape on your stamp.

4 Turn the block over and press down firmly onto white paper. Gently peel away the card to reveal the snake.

5 Let your snake image dry, then add highlights, such as the eyes, with white paint and a fine paintbrush.

▲ You can use your stamp over and over again!

5

Lake City

B y 1325 C.E., the Aztecs were powerful enough to build a capital city, Tenochtitlan (Teh-nosh-teet-lahn). It stood on an island in the middle of a lake and was linked to the shore by four massive **causeways** made from pounded earth. A network of canals ran through the city, and people traveled in small boats along them. Fresh water was carried from nearby mountains into the town by a stone **aqueduct**.

In Aztec legend, the god Huitzilopochtli (Weet-zeel-oh-posh-tlee) told the Aztecs to build their city where they found an eagle sitting on a cactus, eating a snake.

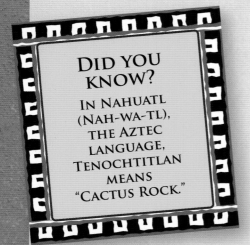

DID YOU KNOW?

IN NAHUATL (NAH-WA-TL), THE AZTEC LANGUAGE, TENOCHTITLAN MEANS "CACTUS ROCK."

CAPITAL CITY

Tenochtitlan grew fast and became one of the largest cities in the world. By 1500 C.E., it was home to over 200 000 people. European explorers said it was cleaner and better than many of their own cities. It was made up of four **districts** called Herons' Home, Flowery Place, Sacred Precinct, and Mosquito Fen.

SACRED PRECINCT

The Sacred Precinct was at the center of the city. The Aztecs believed it was a holy place and built huge temples there. Nearby stood the emperor's vast palace, surrounded by beautiful gardens and a noisy zoo. There were also sports courts for ball games. Ordinary families lived around the outer edge of the city.

Giant stone statues stood at the foot of the steps leading up to the Great Temple in the Sacred Precinct.

MAKE A
GREAT TEMPLE STATUE

The Aztecs carved huge stone statues to stand guard outside their temples. Make an Aztec statue to stand outside your room!

YOU WILL NEED:
BIG BOX • OLD PHONE BOOKS • TAPE • SPARE CARDBOARD • PENCIL • RULER • SHOE BOX • TWO MEDIUM BOXES • PAINT • BIG PAINTBRUSH • BLACK MARKER

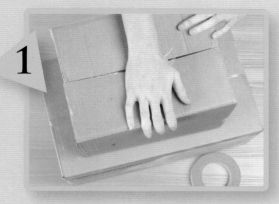

1 Fill the big box with old phone books to weigh it down. Tape it closed. Tape two medium boxes on top.

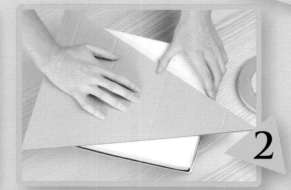

2 Draw a triangle on cardboard. Ask an adult to cut it out. Tape the triangle to the shoe box as shown.

3 Tape the shoe box to the top of the column. Then paint the column with stone-colored paint using a big paintbrush.

Your gigantic statue is sure to impress your friends and family!

4 Once it's dry, draw on the statue's face, arms, legs, and loin cloth. Go over the lines with a black marker.

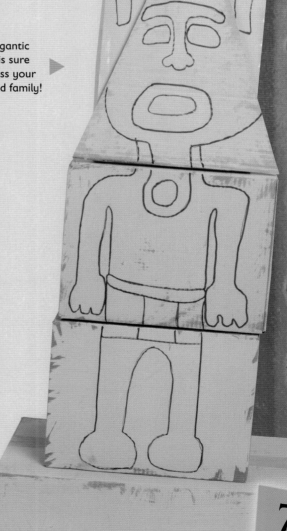

7

CHILLIES AND CHINAMPAS

Aztec farmers had to be inventive because Mesoamerica was not an easy place to grow food. The weather was extreme, especially in the mountains. Summers were baking hot, winters were cold and foggy, and rainfall was unreliable. The Aztecs' main crop was maize (sweet corn). They planted it on mountain slopes and also on artificial islands called chinampas (shee-nam-pahs). These floating gardens were made of branches with mud and stones on top. They were built beside the marshy shores of the lake.

The roots of trees growing on chinampas held the soil together. These farmers (front left) are using an Aztec digging stick, called a uictli (wheek-tlee).

COLORFUL CROPS
On chinampas, farmers grew pumpkins, peppers, chillies, tomatoes, avocados, beans, and peanuts. In a good year, they could produce seven harvests. The Aztec government controlled what was grown to make sure that there was a steady supply of food into the city.

DID YOU KNOW?
HUMAN POO MADE EXCELLENT MANURE TO HELP CROPS GROW. FARMERS COLLECTED THE POO FROM PUBLIC TOILETS IN HUTS BESIDE THE CANALS!

A VARIED DIET
Aztec men hunted wild creatures for food, including deer, rabbits, ducks, and geese. They used nets and hooks to catch fish from the lake. Boys searched for lizards, insects, grubs, worms, mushrooms, and cactus leaves to eat. They also gathered blue-**algae** that grew on shallow water—it tasted like cheese. Hunters killed wild birds for their bright feathers and **jaguar** cats for their spotted skins.

The rain god Tlaloc (Tlah-lock) was known as "He Who Makes Things Grow." The Aztecs worshipped him because without rain, there would be no crops.

8

Make a Rain God Pendant

Aztec jewelry designs often featured gods. Make a pendant of Tlaloc, the god of rain and good harvests, in a few simple steps.

YOU WILL NEED:
AIR-DRYING CLAY • ROLLING PIN • TRACING PAPER • PENCIL • SCISSORS • MODELING TOOL • ACRYLIC PAINTS • PAINTBRUSHES • STRING

1

Warm the clay in your hands for a few moments and then roll out a slab that's about 1/3 in. (1 cm) thick.

2

Trace the image of Tlaloc from the opposite page. Cut your tracing out and place on the clay.

3

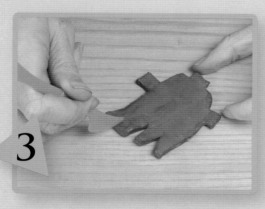

With a modeling tool, cut around your tracing. Cut zigzags along the top to make his crown.

4

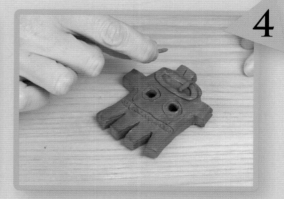

Use a pencil to make two eye holes right through the clay. Add his nose, mouth, and teeth.

5

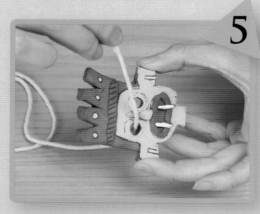

When your pendant is dry, paint it bright colors. Once the paint is dry, thread string through the eyes.

Knot the string and wear! ▶

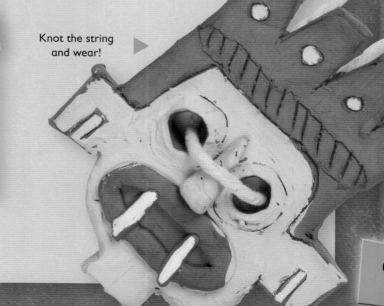

9

FOOD AND SHELTER

Families ate two meals a day, one at noon and one in the evening. Ordinary people ate a mostly vegetarian diet because meat was very expensive. The food was simple. All meals were based on maize. It was crushed and stewed as porridge or ground into flour and mixed with water to make dumplings and thin pancakes (today, called tortillas). Both were served with stewed vegetables, often spiced with hot chillies.

Tortillas were cooked on a hot, flat stone over an open fire. The Aztecs ate with their fingers or scooped up food with tortillas.

Maize flour was made from dried, ground-up maize (sweet corn) grains.

DRINK AZTEC HOT CHOCOLATE

Sip the delicious chocolate drink that only important nobles were allowed to enjoy in Aztec times. Ask an adult to help!

YOU WILL NEED:
4 TBSP COCOA POWDER •
1 CUP MILK • HONEY •
VANILLA EXTRACT • MUG
• MEASURING PITCHER
• SMALL SAUCEPAN • WHISK

1 Put the cocoa powder, a little of the milk, 1 tsp honey, and a few vanilla drops in the pitcher. Stir.

3 Let the adult slowly pour the hot milk onto your cocoa mixture.

GIFTS FOR THE GODS
IN THEIR HOMES, MOST AZTECS HAD A SMALL SHRINE TO THE GODS. FAMILIES PUT OFFERINGS OF FOOD, FLOWERS, OR DROPS OF BLOOD THERE TO PLEASE THEIR GODS.

DRINKS

The Aztecs mainly drank water but on special occasions, beer made from cactus sap was served. Rich people sometimes drank hot chocolate. This was made from rain forest cacao tree beans that were carried to Aztec lands by traders.

DID YOU KNOW?
IT WAS RUDE TO EAT OR DRINK TOO MUCH, AND ALCOHOLICS WERE PUNISHED BY DEATH.

LIFE AT HOME

Most Aztec houses were small. They had one room with an open fire, a courtyard, and a small bathroom. The fire was used for cooking and was never allowed to go out. House walls were built of dried mud bricks and the roofs were thatched with straw. Inside, there was not much furniture—Aztec people sat and slept on woven reed mats on the floor.

Aztecs made a chocolate drink by boiling crushed cacao beans in water. To make it frothy, they poured it from high up.

2

Ask an adult to gently heat the rest of the milk in a saucepan until it is almost bubbling.

Let your hot chocolate cool down slightly before you enjoy drinking it!

4

Use a whisk to whip it up until it's frothy. Pour into a mug!

11

FAMILY LIFE

All Aztec families belonged to a **clan**, called a calpulli (kal-pull-ee). Each calpulli organized its own affairs, from building schools to punishing members who broke the law. Within each family, men, women, and children worked hard to support each other. Everyone had their own responsibilities. Men grew food, built houses, and made useful things. Women cooked, wove cloth, and cared for children and sick relatives.

Women used backstrap looms to weave cloth. The loom was tied to a post and a strap went around the weaver's waist.

DID YOU KNOW?
AT AN AZTEC WEDDING, THE BRIDE WAS CARRIED TO THE GROOM'S FAMILY HOUSE ON THE MATCHMAKER'S BACK.

From the age of six, children started to learn useful skills, such as hunting, weaving, and housecleaning, by watching and helping their parents. Aztec parents were strict. Boys and girls were expected to be obedient and respectful.

MATCHMAKING AND MARRIAGE
Grandparents passed on knowledge, experience, and advice. Young people lived at home until they married, usually at the age of 20. Then the couple lived with the groom's parents and worked for his family. Many marriages were arranged by old women who worked as **matchmakers**.

GOOD NEIGHBORS
When there was a wedding, neighbors gathered for singing, dancing, and a feast. But the Aztecs didn't need a special occasion to relax together. Aztec families lived close to one another and met to talk and play games, such as patolli.

A patolli board had 52 squares, one for each year in the Aztec "century." The Aztecs played to win, and some players bet everything they had on the result of the game.

PLAY PATOLLI

Try your hand at this exciting Aztec board game!

HOW TO PLAY

RULES FOR FOUR PLAYERS

Your aim is to get as many of your beans into the opposite player's base as you can. Take turns rolling the dice. When you throw a six, move onto your base and up the board. Roll again and move one counter at a time up the board. You can move forward and sideways, but not diagonally. If you land on a square with one of your opponent's beans already inside, it's yours. Whoever gets the most beans across the board without being captured, wins!

YOU WILL NEED:
16 x 16 IN. (42 X 42 CM) SQUARE THICK CARDSTOCK • RULER • PENCIL • FELT TIP PEN • COMPASS • PAINT AND BRUSHES OR FELT TIP PENS • 6 MATCHING JELLY BEANS PER PLAYER • DICE

1

Mark the middle of each side of the square. In pencil, join up the marks to make a cross.

2

From the center outward, mark seven 3/4 in. (2 cm) intervals along all four "arms" of the cross.

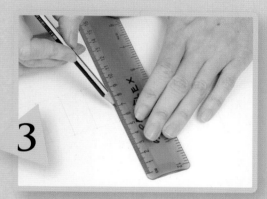

3

Draw a line on either side of both "arms" of the cross that is 3/4 in. (2 cm) away from the crossed lines.

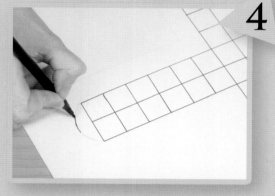

4

Use your marks to draw six lines across each "arm." Add semicircles at the ends. Go over the board in pen.

5

Set your compass to 1 1/2 in. (4 cm). Draw a circle in each corner of the board. Decorate in four colors.

Keep your counters in your "home zone" until you throw a six. Counters you've won from your opponent can also be kept in your home zone!

BASE

HOME ZONE

13

SCHOOL AND STUDY

At 14 years old, boys and girls had to go to school to learn to be good citizens. Most went to local classes called tepochalli (teh-posh-kall-ee). They studied history and religion, traditional songs, and simple counting. Boys also learned to march, obey orders, fight, and handle weapons. They had to be ready to serve in the Aztec army.

Pupils arriving at a tepochalli. ▶

DID YOU KNOW?

EVERY 52 YEARS, THE FARMERS' CALENDAR AND THE HOLY CALENDAR ENDED ON THE SAME DAY. THIS MARKED THE END OF AN AZTEC "CENTURY."

SCHOOL DAYS

Boys from noble families went to high schools called calmecac (kal-mesh-ak). They learned to be priests or government leaders. They studied law, and how to read and write Aztec picture symbols. They also learned how to measure time, using the Aztecs' own special calendars.

AZTEC CALENDARS

The Aztecs measured time in several different ways. Farmers used the sun calendar. It had 360 days, plus five extra. Priests and scribes used the holy calendar. It had 13 months, each with 20 days.

The 20 days of the holy calendar were named after creatures, everyday objects, and powerful forces in the Aztec world.
▼

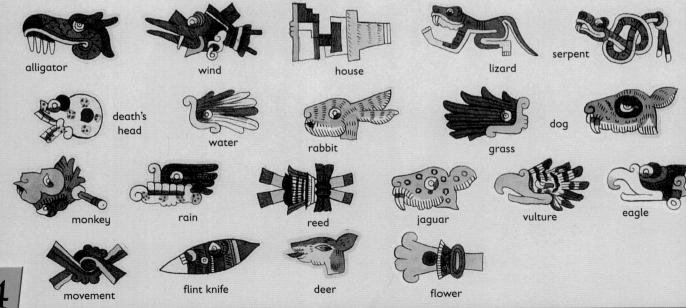

alligator   wind   house   lizard   serpent

death's head   water   rabbit   grass   dog

monkey   rain   reed   jaguar   vulture   eagle

movement   flint knife   deer   flower

14

MAKE AN AZTEC CALENDAR

Learn to measure time like an Aztec! Set the number 1 opposite the alligator. Then turn each wheel clockwise once a day to find the date's name and number.

YOU WILL NEED:
COMPASS • 2 LARGE SHEETS OF WHITE CARDSTOCK (ABOUT 20 x 10 IN. (50 x 20 CM)) • PENCIL • COLORED FELT TIP PENS OR PAINTS AND PAINTBRUSHES • 2 PAPER FASTENERS

1

Set the compass to 1 1/2 in. (4 cm) and draw a circle on the cardstock. Reset the compass to 4 in. (10 cm). Repeat. Cut the circles out.

2

Write 1–13 around the edge of the small circle. Copy or trace all the picture symbols onto the big circle.

3

On the other sheet of cardstock, draw a line across the middle. Mark 3 in. (7 cm) and then 8 1/2 in. (22 cm) from the left edge.

4

Use a sharp pencil to make a hole in the center of each circle and on the two marks on the card.

5

Use paper fasteners to attach the circles to the card. Write on "Months," "Days," and "Today" as shown right.

Each day in the holy calendar had a name and a number. This was repeated only once each 260 days (the Aztec holy calendar year). Is it Two Lizard day today?

TODAY

DAYS

MONTHS

15

TREASURES!

The Aztecs were amazingly skilled craftworkers. They had no machines to help them, no strong iron tools, and no potters' wheels. Using just their hands and simple equipment, such as stone knives and wooden **mallets**, they made magnificent fans, masks, weapons, statues, jewels, and stone carvings. Craft skills were passed down from parents to children, and children started learning young.

DIFFERENT DISTRICTS

Craftworkers lived and worked together in small communities. Different trades, such as goldsmiths or stonemasons, lived in particular areas of the city.

WEAR MOCTEZUMA'S HEADDRESS

Aztec rulers wore splendid headdresses made of priceless feathers and gold. Now you can wear one, too!

Making a feather fan (left) and a feather headdress (right).

YOU WILL NEED:
COMPASS • CARDSTOCK • PENCIL • RULER • SCISSORS • PAINT AND PAINTBRUSHES • GOLD GLITTER GLUE • GREEN, BLUE, AND TURQUOISE PAPER • TAPE

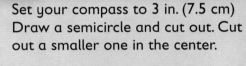

1

Set your compass to 3 in. (7.5 cm) Draw a semicircle and cut out. Cut out a smaller one in the center.

This headdress probably belonged to the great Aztec ruler, Moctezuma (Mock-th-zoh-mah).

4

Tape each of the feathers around the back of the mask. Try to alternate the colors.

FABULOUS FEATHERS

Feather-working was a traditional trade. The Aztecs got brightly colored feathers from hunters who lived in the rain forests. The best feathers, from the blue-green **quetzal** bird, were more valuable than gold. Feather-workers turned them into fans and headdresses and sewed them onto cloaks in elaborate patterns.

ONLY THE FINEST

Owning fine objects displayed **rank** and power. Only nobles and rulers were allowed to have the finest pottery, goldwork, fabric, and fans. Sometimes the Aztecs asked other Mesoamericans, such as the Mixtecs who were master potters, to make goods for them.

Ask an adult or friend to help you tape the ends of the card strip together at the back. Add a centerpiece, as shown, if you like. ▶

2

Paint on stripes of blue, green, and brown for feathers. When dry, add dots of gold using glitter glue.

3

Make a feather template. Use it to draw and cut out 12 feathers from some blue and green paper.

5

Cut out a card strip long enough to go around your head with an overlap of 1 in. (2 cm). Glue headdress to the strip.

DID YOU KNOW?

OBSIDIAN, A GLASSY BLACK STONE, WAS USED BY TOP AZTEC CRAFTWORKERS TO MAKE MIRRORS AND RAZOR-SHARP ARROWHEADS. BUT OBSIDIAN WASN'T EASY TO FIND—IT WAS ONLY MADE BY EXPLODING VOLCANOES!

CLOTHES AND JEWELRY

Clothes showed an Aztec's place in society. By law, ordinary people had to be simply dressed in plain, rough fabric made from cactus fiber. Only nobles were allowed to wear softer cotton, patterned cloaks, and eye-catching jewelry.

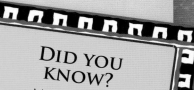

An Aztec nobleman and his wife in fine clothes. He wears a feather pendant; she has a necklace of shells. Both are wearing sandals with decorative laces.

Big, chunky necklaces and bracelets were made from gold.

FASHIONABLE CLOTHES
Most clothes were simply lengths of cloth that were wrapped around the body and tied in place. Women wore **tunics**, like ponchos, over long skirts. Men wore cloaks tied at the shoulder. Both men and women wore heavy, gold or **jade** jewelry —if they were rich enough. Some had pierced lips and ears. Among ordinary people, tattoos and body paint were popular, cheap alternatives to jewelry.

HAIRSTYLES
Unmarried girls wore their hair loose. Married women braided their hair and pinned the braids on top of their heads, like horns. Boys had long hair until they had captured an enemy in battle. Only then were they allowed to cut their hair to shoulder length, like grown men.

Only nobles, or soldiers whose legs had been badly scarred in battle, were allowed to wear cloaks that reached below their knees.

MAKE AN
AZTEC NOBLE'S CLOAK

Your Aztec cloak will remind everyone that you're a very important person. Remember to put on your ankle ornaments, too!

YOU WILL NEED:
35 × 45 IN. (90 × 120 CM) WHITE FABRIC • POSTER OR FABRIC PAINTS • PAINTBRUSHES • PENCIL • 60 IN. (150 CM) PIECE OF RED RIBBON • SCISSORS • GLUE • COMPASS • YELLOW CARDSTOCK • TWO 8 IN. (20 CM) PIECES OF WHITE RIBBON

1

Draw a margin around the edge of the fabric. Draw another line inside it. Add circles around the edge.

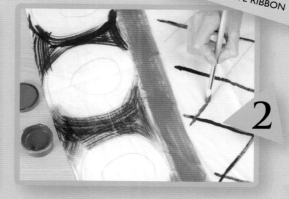 **2**

Paint the inner margin red and the gaps between the circles blue. Add blue crisscrosses.

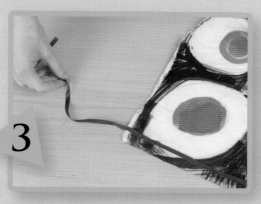 **3**

Put on your cloak and tie the ribbons. Tie the white ribbon strips around your ankles—now you look like a real Aztec!

Paint a red dot inside each circle. Once the paint is dry, glue red ribbon along one short edge. Allow extra at each end.

 **4**

Cut out eight circles from yellow cardstock. Glue four evenly spaced circles along each of your ribbon strips.

AT THE MARKET

Buyers and sellers hoped to get a good deal at the market.

All Aztec towns and cities had a marketplace. Merchants, craftworkers, and farmers met there to **barter** (exchange) goods. Aztecs did not have coins. Instead, they used valuable items such as cacao beans or feathers as money.

DID YOU KNOW?
TRAVELING MERCHANTS WALKED BAREFOOT AS FAR AS 30 MILES (48 KM) A DAY TO BRING GOODS TO SELL AT MARKETS.

BUSTLING MARKET
Most market traders were women. They set up stalls to sell goods produced by their families, such as vegetables, flowers, cloth, mats, and pots. Foreign traders brought gold dust and seashells from the coast or animal skins and feathers from the rain forest. Government officials also sold valuable goods that they had claimed as tribute (tax) from people they had conquered.

TLATELOLCO CITY
In 1473 C.E. the Aztecs conquered the nearby city of Tlatelolco (Tlah-teh-loll-coh) and it became the greatest trading place in Mesoamerica. The Aztecs had no wheeled transport or horses. Porters and merchants carried goods on their backs for hundreds of miles. Merchants traveled so much and met so many different people that Aztec rulers sometimes used them as spies.

Aztec traders brought this monkey pot from the city of Texcoco to sell. It is carved from shiny black obsidian (stone produced by erupting volcanoes).

Make a Monkey Pot

Make a clay pot using the same coil technique as the Aztecs. Ozomatli (Oh-zoh-maht-lee), the Monkey god, protected art, games, and fun.

1 Shape the clay into balls. Then use your hands to roll out the balls into several long thin "sausages."

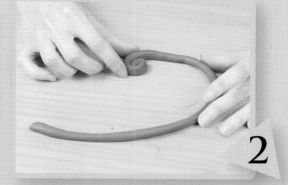

2 Fold in one end of the first sausage and then coil the rest around and around to build up the pot.

3 If you need to add another sausage, just blend the end on. When the pot is big enough, smooth the sides.

4 Roll a dime-sized ball of clay for the head and four small sausages for the feet. Shape the head and feet.

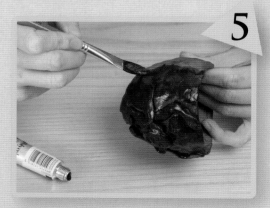

5 Attach the head and feet to the pot and smooth the joins. When the clay has dried, paint it black.

To make your pot shine, use a clean brush to add a layer of PVA mixture (mix three parts PVA to one part water).

READY FOR WAR

The Aztecs were always ready for war and had a well-organized army. They attacked and conquered neighboring countries, took their land, and then demanded tribute (tax) from them. They also took people captive and made them slaves.

Warriors tried to capture enemies alive so that priests could kill them later, as **sacrifices**.

SHOWING COURAGE

Aztec people admired warriors. Young men had to join the army at the age of 17. To show his strength, each ruler had to start his **reign** with a battle. The Aztecs believed it was better to live a short, brave life and die in battle, than **surrender** or retreat. Top warriors were called eagle or jaguar knights.

DRESS UP AS AN AZTEC WARRIOR

Warriors wore real jaguar skins to show that they shared the strength and fierceness of a big cat. Make a frightening, fake jaguar skin.

YOU WILL NEED:
WHITE COTTON FABRIC • SEWING SCISSORS • PENCIL • BLACK MARKER • ACRYLIC OR POSTER PAINTS • PAINTBRUSHES • TWO PIECES OF RED RIBBON

1

Fold the fabric diagonally to make a large triangle. Now cut along the fold.

Put on your jaguar cloak and feel strong and brave, just like an Aztec warrior.

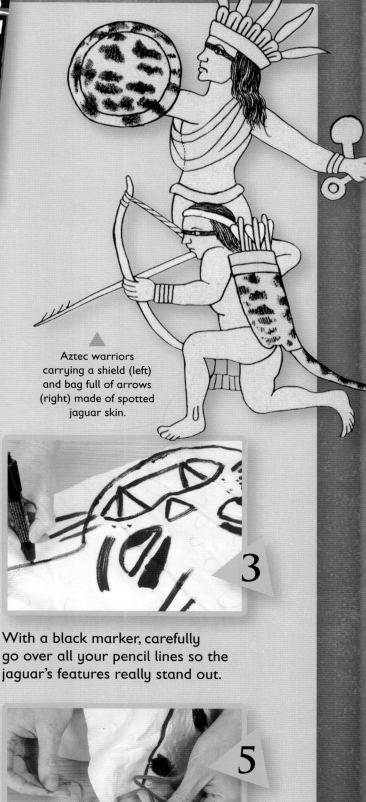

Aztec warriors carrying a shield (left) and bag full of arrows (right) made of spotted jaguar skin.

WEAPONS AND ARMOR

Aztec warriors were armed with wooden spears and clubs tipped with razor-sharp flakes of **flint**. Their armor was made of quilted cotton soaked in salty water. This made it surprisingly tough and strong. For extra protection, warriors carried around wood or leather shields: the finest were trimmed with fur or feathers.

2

In pencil, draw on the body, tail, front legs, and head. Draw dots all over your jaguar's body.

With a black marker, carefully go over all your pencil lines so the jaguar's features really stand out.

3

4

Mix up orange paint and color in the jaguar. Don't go over the black lines! Add the spots with black marker.

5

With scissors, cut a tiny hole on each side of the jaguar's head. Thread red ribbon through each of the holes.

23

KNOW YOUR PLACE

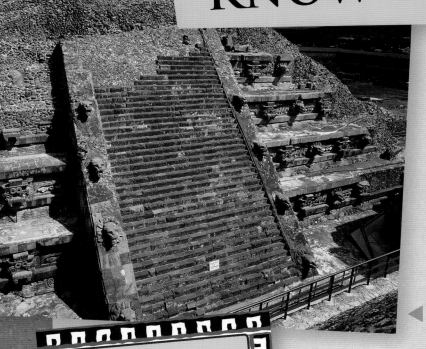

The Aztecs thought that gods controlled everything in the universe including the sun, wind, rain, growing crops, families, travelers, death, disease, and war. They believed that their leader was **descended** from a god. The Aztecs built stepped pyramids with temples at the top. These mountain-like buildings were designed to rise above the earth so the Aztecs were closer to the gods.

No Aztec pyramid temples have survived. But they would have looked like this pyramid, built by earlier Mexican people in the city of Teotihuacan.

DID YOU KNOW?

AN ORDINARY PERSON WISHING TO SPEAK TO A RULER AT THE PALACE HAD TO KEEP THEIR EYES LOOKING DOWN AND BOW VERY LOW. WHEN THEY LEFT, THEY WALKED BACKWARD BECAUSE IT WAS VERY RUDE TO FACE AWAY FROM THE RULER.

RULERS AND GOVERNMENT

The leader of the Aztecs was called the Speaker and his deputy was the Snake woman. They were all-powerful. The Speaker made laws and was head of the army. The Snake woman ran the government. At the start of the Aztec civilization, rulers were chosen from the best warriors. Eventually this changed and they were chosen only from the last ruler's family.

This mask is of the god Tezcatlipoca (Tess-kah-tlee-poh-ka). It is a real skull covered in a mosaic of semiprecious stones.

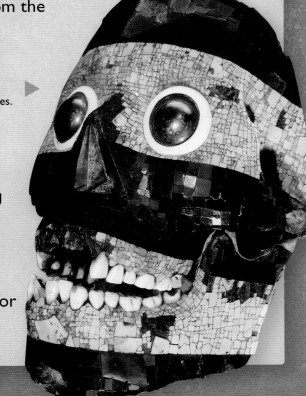

LAW AND ORDER

Rulers were surrounded by a **ruling class** of well-trained officials, priests, noblemen, judges, and scribes. But most Aztecs were poor, ordinary folk known as "macehuatlin" (mah-shee-wat-lin). Below them came slaves, who were prisoners of war, criminals, or very poor people. Ordinary peoples' lives were strictly controlled by tough Aztec laws and harsh punishments. The penalty for many crimes was death, beating, or torture.

MAKE AN AZTEC MASK

This death mask is guaranteed to frighten your friends. Tezcatlipoca was the god of night and the future. Aztecs believed he started wars.

YOU WILL NEED:
A PIECE OF BLACK CARDSTOCK
• RULER • PENCIL • SCISSORS
• CRAFT KNIFE • SILVER FOIL
• BLUE, GREEN, TURQUOISE, BLACK, AND WHITE PAPER
• GLUE • ELASTIC THREAD •
WHITE FELT OR CARDSTOCK

1 Measure your face. On the cardstock, draw an oval shape that is big enough to completely cover your face.

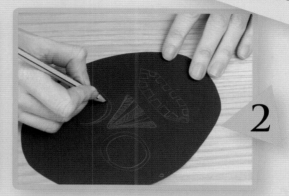

2 Draw on the eyes, mouth, and nose. Then ask an adult to cut them out with a craft knife.

3 Glue on two wide strips of foil. Cut out the eyes, nose, and mouth holes. Glue on colored paper shapes.

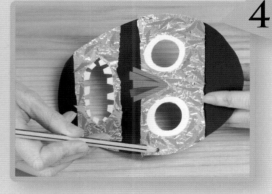

4 Use a sharp pencil to make holes for the elastic at each side of the mask, below the eyes.

5 Finally, thread elastic through the side holes. Put the mask on. Gently tighten the elastic and knot it to secure the mask.

Put on your mask and imagine that you can see into the future, like a god.

CEREMONIES AND SACRIFICES

Religious ceremonies were an essential part of Aztec life. They linked people to the mighty gods. The Aztecs **worshiped** by saying prayers, singing, dancing, and offering flowers, incense, and gold.

In the game "volador," four men tied to ropes jumped from a tall pole. They tried to fly around, like the sun moving across the sky. They aimed to make 52 turns, one for each year in an Aztec century.

DID YOU KNOW?

EUROPEAN TRAVELERS CLAIMED THAT THE AZTECS ATE FLESH FROM SACRIFICED CAPTIVES. THIS MAY BE TRUE—WE DO NOT KNOW—BUT IT PROBABLY DID NOT HAPPEN OFTEN.

THE LAST WORLD

Aztecs thought that the world had been created, then destroyed, four times before. They were living in the fifth world—and it was the final one! To stop their world from coming to an end, Aztec men and women "fed" the gods with life-giving blood. They pricked their earlobes every day, to produce two drops as an offering. At holy festivals, they sacrificed hundreds of humans, mostly prisoners of war, to the gods.

DON'T TRY THIS AT HOME

HUMAN SACRIFICE

The ideal sacrifice was male, young, brave, strong, and handsome. In Aztec eyes, this was the most valuable kind of person. Aztec priests killed victims at the top of temple steps by cutting out their hearts and letting their blood flow down. Winners of sports were also often sacrificed! They had a religious purpose—to help keep the world alive.

Aztec musicians play a leather-topped drum (left) and a hollow wooden drum (center) while dancers shake rattles and wave fans.

MAKE AN AZTEC RATTLE

Whistles, rattles, and drums were played by musicians at ceremonies. Make your own rattle and try it out!

Blow up your balloon and cover it in jelly. Dip strips of newspaper in the PVA mixture and cover the balloon.

When dry, pop the balloon and remove it. Carefully pour raw lentils in through the hole.

Push the rod into the rattle. Keep it upright and put lots of small strips of masking tape around hole and rod.

Paint your rattle brown. When the paint is dry, add zigzags and dots. Then tape two feathers to the top.

▲
Shake your rattle while your friend taps out a rhythm on a table top!

THE END OF THE WORLD?

In spite of making sacrifices to their gods, the Aztecs were still fearful. Ancient legends told how the snake god Quetzalcoatl would arrive and bring the world to an end. The Aztecs expected to see strange signs before he arrived and, in 1519 C.E., this seemed to be happening. Aztec ruler Moctezuma had nightmares about the future. Priests saw **eclipses** of the sun and a blazing **comet**. Monstrous four-legged men were reported.

At first, the Aztecs greeted Europeans peacefully. They did not realize that the Europeans wanted their land.

MAKE A FOLDING CODEX

The Aztecs recorded their history by writing with picture symbols in folding books called codexes. Find out how to make your own.

YOU WILL NEED:
LARGE SHEET OF THIN WHITE CARDSTOCK • RULER • PENCIL • COLORED PENCILS

1

Cut a 50 x 10 in. (125 x 25 cm) strip of cardstock. Measure, then draw four lines on the strip, 10 in. (25 cm) apart.

3

Starting at the back, in the top right-hand corner, draw picture symbols (see p. 29) into the codex.

Historians have learned a lot about Aztec life by reading codexes that have survived. The Aztecs started writing at the back of each codex, in the top right-hand corner.

THE SPANISH ARRIVE

In fact, a Spanish explorer named Hernán Cortés had landed on the Mesoamerican coast. He came in search of treasure. The "monsters" were his men riding horses; the Aztecs had never seen them before. Cortés and his men marched toward Tenochtitlan, helped by the Aztecs' enemies. Many peoples that the Aztecs had conquered now wanted to see them destroyed.

THE END OF THE AZTECS

In 1520 C.E., the Aztecs drove Cortés away, but Moctezuma was killed. The next year, Cortés returned. He destroyed the city and killed most of its citizens. Within 100 years, European diseases that the Spanish brought with them had almost wiped out the Aztec people and their fascinating civilization.

> ### DID YOU KNOW?
> CODEX PAINTERS WERE HIGHLY THOUGHT OF. THEY WERE KNOWN AS TLACUILO (TLAH-KHWEE- LOH) WHICH MEANS "PUTTER DOWN OF THOUGHTS."

2

Line your ruler up with the first line and make a fold. Use this method to fold the strip into an accordian.

4

Color in your picture symbols using colored pencils. You could go over them in black marker, too.

You could design your own picture symbols showing some of the things you do and see every day. ▶

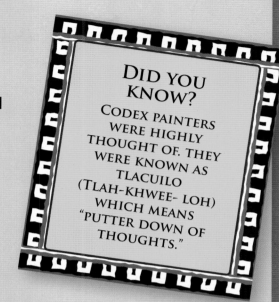

algae Simple life-forms, related to animals, plants, and bacteria. Often they appear as slime or seaweed.

aqueduct A high bridge specially designed to carry water over land.

barter Exchange goods for others of equal value.

causeway Road raised above the surrounding ground on a mound of earth or stones.

clan Group of families that share the same ancestors.

comet A ball of ice and dust that travels though space.

descended To be related to your ancestors. You are descended from your parents and grandparents.

districts Specific areas within a big city or large area of countryside.

dominated Ruled over or controlled by.

eclipse (solar) When the Moon passes in front of the sun, blocking out its light.

flint A hard rock that can be made into a sharp cutting edge.

jade A precious stone that is pale green, shiny, and hard.

jaguar Large, fierce wild cat with spotted skin.

mallet Wooden hammer.

matchmaker Person who finds partners for single people to marry.

Maya Mesoamerican people who built cities in the rain forests. Most powerful between 300–900 C.E.

quetzal Rain forest bird with beautiful green feathers.

rank A person's place in society.

reign Length of time that a ruler stays in power.

ruling class Powerful group in a society that controls other people in the same society.

sacrifice Killing people or animals to please the gods.

surrender Give up and hand over power.

Toltec Mesoamerican people who ruled the Central Valley of Mexico from around 900–1200 C.E.

tunic Long, straight piece of clothing with no sleeves.

worship To respect or love a god or goddess.

INDEX

• The Aztecs loved music and dancing. The children can listen to the sound of Aztec music at http://www.princetonartmuseum.org/Jaguar/jaguar.html and http://www.mexicolore.co.uk/index.php?one=azt&two.aaa Encourage the children to copy some Aztec sounds and rhythms on drums, recorders, or any other instruments that they can play.

• The Aztecs believed that they could see a giant rabbit on the surface of the moon. Take your child outside one dark night when the moon is full. You can find a picture of the rabbit and read an Aztec legend about the moon at http://www.adlerplanetarium.org/cyberspace/moon/culture.html. Do not allow your child to go out at night unaccompanied.

• Research some Aztec stories. For example, Star Snake is the hero of an exciting story written by Martin Auer, from Austria, in 2000. You can find Star Snake's story online at http://www.mexconnect.com/mex_/travel/kmetzger/kmstarsnake.html. Read this, or another story, to the children. Ask them to first imagine themselves as Aztecs and then to write their own story.

• Many Aztec customs still survive today. Every year, on October 31st, Mexicans celebrate the Day of the Dead to honor their dead ancestors. Families decorate tombs, hold feasts, join in processions, make skeleton dolls, and eat sweets shaped like skulls! Help the children to make a papier-mâché piñata or skeleton dolls.

• With the children, create an enormous Aztec time line. Research important events in Aztec history in the library or on the Internet (see http://www.metmuseum.org/toah/ht/08/canm/ht08canm.htm). Mark the events and ask the children to draw and color pictures for each significant date.

• The Aztecs used picture symbols for writing numbers, as well as words. Look for reference material on Aztec numbers at the library or on the Internet (try http://www.ancientscripts.com/aztec.html). Create a simple "code book" of numbers and symbols, and photocopy one for each of the children. Then create simple games for the children or ask them to "write" their birth date in picture symbols.

Useful Web sites

Mexicolore is an excellent resource for the study of Mexico and the Aztecs, compiled by teachers and entertainers: http://www.mexicolore.co.uk/index.php.

Children can play Aztec games at: http://www.mesoweb.com/crystal/index.html.

Visit the Web site of a museum near the ruins of the Great Temple in what was Tenochtitlan: http://archaeology.la.asu.edu/tm/index2.php.